TRANSPORT
PHILATELY
SERIES

NARROW GAUGE
RAILWAY
STAMPS

TRANSPORT
PHILATELY
SERIES

NARROW GAUGE
RAILWAY
STAMPS

HOWARD PILTZ

PEN & SWORD
TRANSPORT

First published in Great Britain in 2017 by
Pen & Sword Transport
An imprint of Pen & Sword Books Ltd
47 Church Street
Barnsley
South Yorkshire
S70 2AS

ISBN 9781473871786

Typeset in Cormorant Infant by Pen & Sword Books Ltd
Printed and bound by Replika Press Pvt Ltd.

Pen & Sword Books Ltd incorporates the imprints of Pen & Sword Archaeology,
Atlas, Aviation, Battleground, Discovery, Family History, History, Maritime,
Military, Naval, Politics, Railways, Select, Social History, Transport, True Crime,
and Claymore Press, Frontline Books, Leo Cooper, Praetorian Press, Remember
When, Seaforth Publishing and Wharncliffe.

For a complete list of Pen and Sword titles please contact:
Pen and Sword Books Limited
47 Church Street, Barnsley, South Yorkshire, S70 2AS, England
E-mail: enquiries@pen-and-sword.co.uk
Website: www.pen-and-sword.co.uk

CONTENTS

INTRODUCTION

The two sides

Collecting stamps brings a wonderful new view of the world that the collector – celebrated in the more formal title of the philatelist – is led through an amazing world of knowledge, where the inquisitive mind would ponder some mysteries of bygone times: Why, you may ask, do British postage stamps never, but never boast their country of origin, whilst Swiss ones bear the enigmatic title 'Helvetia' and, as if that is not difficult enough, then where *are* some far-off lands that these days only appear in our history books? Go south a tad, one might be told, to find Southern Rhodesia, or for that matter just a little more thought might be needed to give us the answer for that evocative name Tanganyika.

Likewise, someone with a worldly interest in transport may find that the hobby will lead him – or her – all over the world, if not literally then as a by-product of studying the subject. There are a great many transport professionals who have worked on several different continents throughout their working lives to bring the benefit of their skills to areas one might consider under-developed in the areas of public transport. Personally, the author has spent many years as an enthusiast of most forms of public transport and has been to places that, until the advent of cheap air travel, seemed quite outlandish. Whilst he has never been to Indonesia, he has read, enthralled, of the fire-breathing dragons that abounded there; however, he has been to a lake on Vancouver Island on Canada's Pacific coast where lived the world's two largest flying boats rejoicing in the name of 'Mars', whilst it seemed to him at the time – he was 14 – quite exciting, but utterly easy in 1959, to talk himself onto the inaugural KLM Viscount flight from Manchester to Amsterdam, only to find there was no return flight home that day (memories of the heart-clutching scream from his Dad over the phone will never fade: 'You're WHERE?') or a flight, not much later but this time with permission – and paid for – to go plane-spotting alone to the Paris Air Show. Not many years later, he visited the USA to look for the last gasps of two iconic forms of American transport – PCC trams in Newark, NJ, and the Pennsylvania Railroad GG1 electric locomotives. I could also go on a little too long about getting rather merry drinking the local brews in places like Prague, Lisbon or the countryside around Brussels whilst chasing trams.

Coming Together with Works of Art

At first sight it might seem a little odd that one should wish to combine these two totally disparate hobbies, but by good fortune the author happens to have a liking for both subjects and a long time ago began to appreciate that in stamps one could find the wonderful combination of transport

history told within a glorious gallery of miniature works of art. See through the ages how the reproduction techniques on stamps have developed from simple monochrome etchings with formal, carefully sculpted borders such as this 1954 Fiji example with an illustration of a Leeds-built locomotive and celebrating the islands well-known sugar industry. Interestingly, apart from a very few definitives of the 1890s and 1900's it was to be 1963 before a British stamp would appear with more than one colour; not even the UK's 1953 Coronation stamps boasted more. The accepted appearance developed first to two or three colours and then, as with everything else towards the end of the twentieth century, convention went out of the window as we saw full colour art-work and the use of photographs and quite often in these days of digital photography – fairly heavily manipulated ones at that.

What is in this collection?

There will be several different formats that the reader will find mentioned in this book, and there follows a brief summary for the novice philatelist:

Mint stamps: unused stamps, un-marked on their face and with the gum on the back still intact. It used to be the habit of collectors to stick gummed, paper hinges to the back of their stamps for mounting in an album. The damage that this does for serious collectors has discredited this practice and one will often find these days the initials MNH (Mint, not hinged) within the description of a particular stamp or set of stamps.

Used stamps: As the terminology suggests, postage stamps that have been used for the purpose they were designed for, indicating that the due fee for the service required has been paid, and stuck on the envelope or parcel as proof. Hence, they bear a post-mark (sometimes referred to as a 'franking' or 'cancellation') to indicate the office of cancellation and will undoubtedly have no gum on the back but traces of the paper they had been stuck to. Apart from its rarity value, a collector will look for how heavy the post-mark appears on the stamp and how well the backing has been removed. A thinning of the stamp itself or loss of any part of the face or the perforations will render the stamp valueless, scrap, or – where it is a particularly rare example – seriously devalued.

Definitives: What one could describe as the regular, run-of-the-mill stamps, that one would get over the counter on a day-to-day basis.

Miniature Sheets, or minisheets are often produced by the issuing postal authority using either one stamp with a border that might be an extension of the illustration on the stamp, or several stamps within that border, surrounded by a description.

FFESTINIOG RAILWAY COMPANY
RAILWAY LETTER STAMPS

Designed by S R Hudson . Printed by Walsall Security Printers

1254

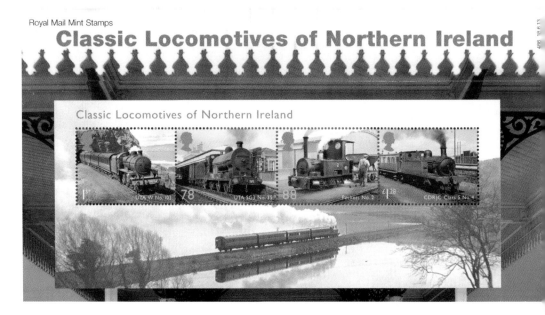

Classic Locomotives of Northern Ireland

Classic Locomotives of Northern Ireland

Presentation packs: Here we have one of the philatelist's best friends, for not only is there usually one, pristine and mint example of each stamp in any particular issue but they are presented behind a clear film, hinged so that the stamps may be withdrawn if one wishes, within a card wallet often containing sometimes quite copious details of the event celebrated as well as technical information, all within a cellophane envelope for virtually indefinite preservation. Look at the illustration above on the Northern Ireland set where the author has used information on the locomotives from the copious notes that are part of the pack.

First Day Cover (FDC): If the Presentation Pack is not your thing then join the many collectors of the FDC, as its name implies, posted and franked on the first day the stamps go into circulation and so gaining a certain cachet. The envelope, or cover, may be a product of the issuing post office and cancelled with a special, carefully applied franking, but that is by no means certain and quite often you may find that a specialist dealer or the organisation involved may have produced their

own cover, obtained the stamps in advance and even having a hand in designing the special franking.

Specialist Covers: These are covers that are not designed for use on the first day of issue of a particular stamp or set of stamps. An organisation, maybe with an eye on the commercial opportunity, will produce a specially printed envelope to commemorate an event, even if no special stamps have been issued, using a postage stamp that may or may not be of particular relevance, and possibly apply a special franking. These are often very attractive and collectable, as this illustration produced by Buckingham

Celebrating Classic
Locomotives of Northern Ireland

Covers of Folkestone, Kent, who have a thriving business producing attractive covers for the collector, in this case adding their own image of one of the Northern Ireland presentation set. They are of value only within a small circle of collectors.

PHQ Cards: 'PHQ' stands for Postal Headquarters but here refers to reproduction of stamps on post-cards; all items published by the British Post Office are given a number that is prefixed by the letters PHQ. The first ever card was the 3p W.G. Grace stamp from the set commemorating County Cricket. Issued on 16th May 1973, this card was numbered PHQ 1 and the numbering sequence has continued to the present day. There are several sets that replicate stamps illustrating our hobby.

Railway Letter Service: The Railway Letter Post was created on 1 February 1891, by agreement between the Postmaster General and seventy-five British railway companies of the era. The original railway letter fee, in addition to the normal Royal Mail postage, was 2d (0.83p). More recently, modern day railway preservation organisations have seen a commercial opportunity and examples of their stamps are illustrated in this book.

What is not generally in the author's collection are stamps produced where there is quite obviously no intention to satisfy a need to provide a postal service in the issuing country. There are, however, a few cases breaking that rule and illustrated are examples of stamps produced for postal authorities in the West Indies by a magazine publisher! As you will see, the end results are worthy of inclusion due to their exemplary quality and of course one has to admit that in a great many cases the railway letter service stamps produced by today's preserved railways are principally produced for sale to collectors.

So, please follow me now on a rather circuitous tour of our world with the aid of the artist and his fascination with transport through the medium of the postage stamp.

NARROW GAUGE RAILWAYS

I first became interested in narrow gauge railways when I was taken to the Talyllyn Railway as a young teenager and approaching the waiting train down the slope at Wharf station the summer sun caught the splash of green and brass, and what came to mind was that adjective so apt but that today always makes my skin crawl; 'cute'!

Is it that same adjective that is such a draw to stamp designers? There seems to be a disproportionate number of narrow gauge subjects that appear on postage stamps from around the world and it is on a survey around that globe that this book will take the reader, not an exhaustive look at each and every country nor a itemisation of every stamp on the subject ever produced – for that take a look at Stanley Gibbons' *Collect Railways on Stamps* – but a browse through the author's collection starting at home, here in the UK. Not a particularly good start, as the Royal Mail didn't discover the subject of narrow gauge railways until

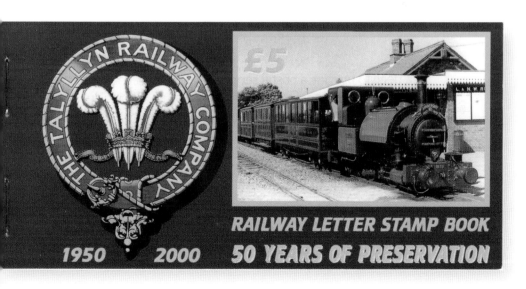

2000, as described in the next chapter. However, since then, there have been several interesting issues including four separate sets between 2011 and 2014 featuring the Classic Locomotives of England, Wales, Scotland and Northern Ireland, again mentioned in the next chapter.

If the Royal Mail ignored the narrow gauge, then the various issuing authorities from the islands around Britain's coast certainly did not. The Isle of Man and Jersey in particular have celebrated their heritage with issue after issue of some of the most handsome works of art in this volume. The various heritage railways have also issued many of their own Railway Letter Service stamps (more correctly known as labels) as well as specially decorated envelopes to mark appropriate occasions.

The Talyllyn Railway was the world's first railway to be resurrected by preservationists and also the first of this modern era to issue railway letter fee stamps on May 23rd 1957 (illustrated below). They were issued in a set of twelve and are now highly prized in any collection.

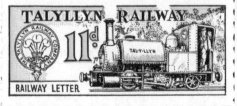

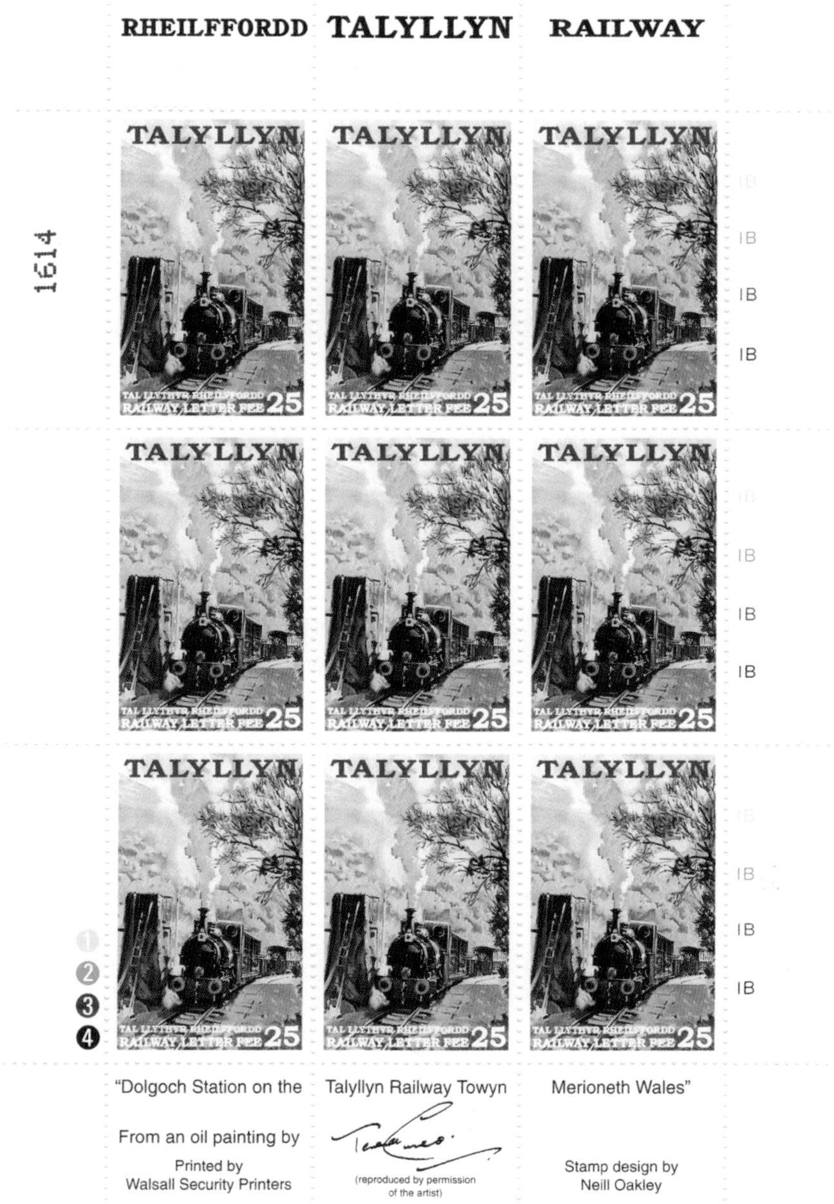

RHEILFFORDD TALYLLYN RAILWAY
TALYLLYN
TAL LLYTHYR RHEILFFORDD
RAILWAY LETTER FEE 25
1614
IB
"Dolgoch Station on the
Talyllyn Railway Towyn
Merioneth Wales"
From an oil painting by
Printed by
Walsall Security Printers
(reproduced by permission
of the artist)
Stamp design by
Neill Oakley

This block of stamps was issued by the Talyllyn Railway in 1996 and shows that most iconic of views, the water-tank at Dolgoch Station, deep in the woods and just after the railway has crossed the deep gorge by the Dolgoch Falls. The view is captured by the brush of one of Great Britain's foremost artists of the modern era Terence Cuneo CVO, OBE, RGI, FGRA., (1907-96). He was famous for his scenes of railways, horses and military action and for the little mouse that featured in all but his earliest works. He was also the official artist for the Coronation of Queen Elizabeth II in 1953

Celebrating the life of
Rev. Wilbert Vere Awdry
16th June 1911 - 21st March 1997
Clergyman, author and supporter of the Talyllyn Railway
Locomotive No.1 "Talyllyn"   Locomotive No.2 "Dolgoch"

"Peter Sam" on the Talyllyn Railway   Locomotive No.7 "Tom Rolt"

Stamps designed and borders illustrated by Neill Oakley   **Talyllyn Railway Vintage Train**   *Printed by Walsall Security Printers*

Amongst several sets of stamps issued by the Talyllyn was this mini-sheets issued in 1998 to celebrate the life of Rev. Wilbert Vere Awdry (1911-97) famed throughout world as the author of the Thomas the Tank Engine series of books first published in 1945 using stories dreamed up to amuse his son Christopher who had been suffering from measles.

Reverend Awdry and his family visited the Talyllyn Railway in 1952, and formed a firm attachment that resulted in five books in this series that described the Skarloey Railway unashamedly based on the Talyllyn as were the engines, and in fact three of the latter have appeared in the Skarloey guise as illustrated on one of these stamps. Christopher Awdry has retained a strong interest in the line and the author is fortunate to have this mini-sheet signed by him.

Then came the Ffestiniog Railway, with a history that goes back to its Incorporation by Act of Parliament in 1832. The line opened in 1836, becoming a party to the Railway Letter Post agreement, as touched upon in the Introduction, on 28 May 1891. However, the FR's connection with the postal

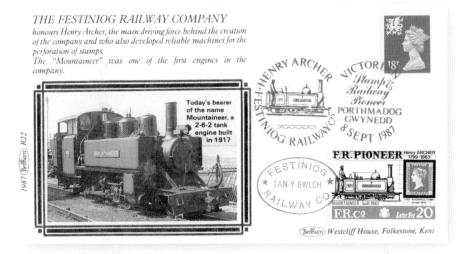

THE FESTINIOG RAILWAY COMPANY
honours Henry Archer, the main driving force behind the creation
of the company and who also developed reliable machines for the
perforation of stamps.
The "Mountaineer" was one of the first engines in the
company.

service extends much further back. The man responsible for raising most of the money needed to build the railway in the 1830s was a Dublin lawyer, Henry Archer, who became a major shareholder and a director of the company. He was

FFESTINIOG RAILWAY COMPANY
RAILWAY LETTER STAMPS

FFESTINIOG RAILWAY COMPANY LOCOMOTIVE BUILT 1928

TAKEN FROM A PHOTOGRAPH LOANED BY THE FR COMPANY ARCHIVES.
DESIGN BY MOORSIDE TYPESETTING AND PRINT MANAGEMENT LTD.
PRINTED BY WALSALL SECURITY PRINTERS LTD.

THE FESTINIOG RAILWAY COMPANY
RAILWAY LETTER STAMPS

Designed by: M. Seymour   Printed by: Faulwood & Herbert Ltd, Brighton

Nº   0332

FFESTINIOG RAILWAY COMPANY
RAILWAY LETTER STAMPS

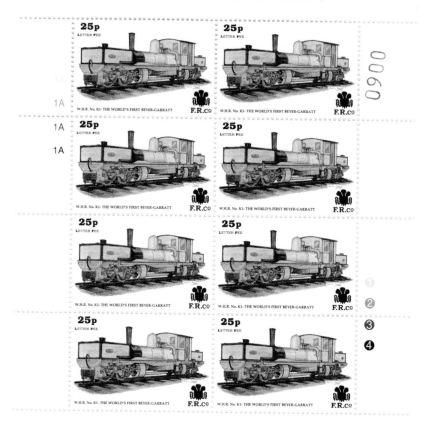

Artwork & design by Edwin Craggs of Moorside Publishing Limited
Printed by Walsall Security Printers Limited

also an inventor and, in 1848, designed one of the earliest practical machines for perforating sheets of postage stamps. He is commemorated on an FR stamp issued in September 1987.

Between 1891 and the late 1930s, the amount of railway letter post carried by the FR did not justify the issuing of special letter fee stamps and payment was collected by the use of a railway parcel stamp on the envelope. The service became dormant with the cessation of FR passenger trains in September 1939 and the subsequent closure of the railway in 1946. Following reopening of the FR from 1955, a copy of the 1891 agreement was found in the archives. Enquiries established that it was still valid and the decision was made to revive the service. It was relaunched on 28 May 1969, when a specially designed set of FR letter fee stamps was issued for the first time. Subsequently, there have been a large number of stamp issues, as well as commemorative first day covers and special cancellations to mark major events in the railway's history.

Whether it is Railway Letter Fee stamps from other railways in the UK and around the world, or conventional postage stamps featuring the narrow gauge, let me lead you through a fascinating world.

THE BRITISH ISLES

The all-inclusive term for the whole of **Great Britain**, the island of Ireland and the islands around those shores is a convenient title for this first chapter, but where to start? Although Great Britain was not the first constituent to issue stamps on the narrow gauge, the Royal Mail discovered our subject in 2000, when in a series of stamps to focus on the beginning of the twenty-first century they looked at several subjects appropriate to the era.

The Welsh Highland Railway was a long moribund railway line that had connected Dinas, just south of Caernarfon in the top-left-corner of North Wales, southish to Porthmadog through the wonderful countryside of Snowdonia. The well-known Ffestiniog Railway took on the monumental task of rebuilding the line and extending it back to within sight of Caernarfon Castle and with numerous other sources, received funding from the

FIRST DAY OF ISSUE

25p
LETTER FEE

F.R.C° W.H.R. GARRATT No. 138

TO BE POSTED ON ARRIVAL
AT DINAS STATION

Celebrating Classic
Locomotives of Wales

Millennium Commission. It was therefore appropriate than one of the line's iconic Beyer-Garratt locomotives was given the name *Millennium*, or, in Welsh, *Mileniwm* (one on each side) and it is this engine that the Royal Mail decided to illustrate.

It was 2014 before the Royal Mail issued any more narrow gauge stamps and this time there were four separate issues 'Celebrating the Classic locomotives of England, Wales, Scotland and Northern Ireland', and on two we were treated to narrow gauge subjects, one of which is illustrated here on a cover by Buckinghams. This lovely cover was based on paintings especially produced by John Wigston GRA (Guild of Railway Artists). From the Wales cover we see the Ffestiniog Railway's well-loved locomotive Blanche and from the Welshpool & Llanfair, *The Earl*, threading the long-lost section of track through the back-streets of Welshpool.

Turning to the islands around Great Britain, it is difficult to decide where to start, for the postal authorities of many have ensured their transport history is well represented on their stamps – one suspects in the case of the **Isle of Man** as an aid to the tourist industry – and by employing talented artists to produce some very colourful images. Whilst their first issue as an independent issuing office was in July 1973, later the same year a small series was issued to mark the Isle of Man Railway. In 1988, a new series of definitives was issued, covering all aspects of the islands rail-bound transport, every element of which can be classified as vintage. Of the sixteen stamps in the series, the four stamps illustrated here on a First Day Cover issued by the IoM Post Office shows three trains from the Isle of Man Railway that originally covered most of the island, and one from the 2-foot gauge Groudle Glen line, situated in a small picturesque glen just north of Douglas that is run as a Manx charity solely operated by volunteers and one of the few lines on the island that wasn't built to the island-standard gauge of 3-feet.

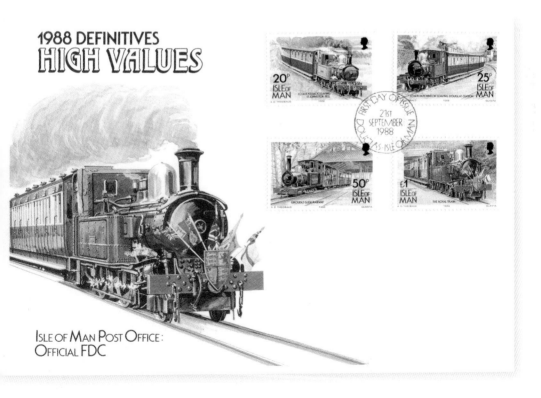

The **Republic of Ireland** was also a big user of the 3-foot gauge, taking advantage of cheaper infrastructure costs to serve many rural and isolated parts of the country. Many lines developed into very important systems, including the County Donegal and Londonderry and Lough Swilly lines, and I have chosen to illustrate a 1995 series of stamps featuring the narrow gauge including a view of the Cork & Muskerry Railway, built originally in 1887 to connect Cork with Blarney to tap the tourist trade. The railway ran alongside the Cork city trams that had amongst its destinations another Blackpool, but whilst the artist has done an amazing job, he seems to have the conductor and passengers sitting above the level of the overhead!

Nearer to France and Continental Europe than to Great Britain are the Channel Isles, the largest and best known of which is **Jersey** which has celebrated its transport heritage with several issues of postage stamps, some featuring the island's two long-lost railways that ran east and west from the island's capital St Helier and this First Day Cover

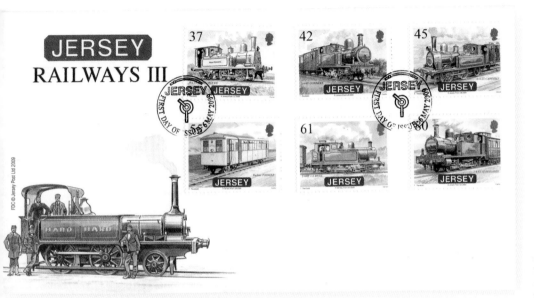

from the island's Post Office is a very attractive souvenir. Interestingly, much of the trackbed of the western line remains in place as footpaths along the promenade to St. Aubin and then through the countryside to Corbiere and its famous lighthouse on a rock outcrop.

The scene is illustrated by this stamp issued in 2013 showing the Grand National winner of 1983, so named because the white blaze on his face resembles the lighthouse. The author has a very large collection of Jersey stamps in Presentation Packs that make a fascinating commentary of the island's history and way of life, and rates them probably amongst the finest in the world.

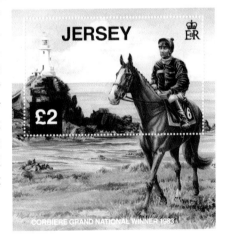

CONTINENTAL EUROPE

It is now just a short hop across the English Channel (or as the French call it – La Manche) to a continent that has enjoyed a huge variation in narrow gauge railways although, as already mentioned, these lines were usually adopted because of their lower infrastructure costs when pushing away from major hubs to less densely populated areas, or where hill-climbing dictated many sinuous curves. So very often we think of these lines at the same time as rural landscapes, beautiful or mountainous scenery ripe for later lives as part of the twentieth and twenty-first century culture of tourism. As soon as motorised road transport became more readily available, these lines were usually amongst the first to perish and very often it is those tourists we must thank for the survival of many lines.

As we have already seen, the inspiration for colourful subjects to illustrate stamps has been appreciated by some nations' postal authorities more than others and so you might look in vain in this book for stamps from such as the Americas as mentioned later.

France is noted worldwide for beautiful design and sophistication so characterised by French fashion but its postage stamps have not majored on transport subjects, although in fact until the twenty-first century few large series of stamps were produced. I have chosen four stamps to illustrate and each one shows a line that has survived thanks principally to the nature of the area it serves.

The first illustration shows a composite illustration of le petit train jaune, (the little yellow train) that bills itself as one of the greatest railway journeys of the world, possibly a slight exaggeration but nevertheless a wonderful journey through the French Pyrenees from its lower terminus at Villefranche de Conflent, about 50kms from Perpignan on the Mediterranean coast, to the other end at Latour de Carol, very close to the Spanish border. The metre-gauge line is entirely

electrified and its rolling stock ranges from the original stock to some recent additions based more on street-tramway practice. Unfortunately, at the time of writing, the line is under something of a cloud regarding its future! It is particularly noticeable that two currencies are quoted on this stamp as it was issued in 2000 around the time the French Franc was being replaced by the Euro

The next stamp, issued in 1993, illustrates le train d'Artouste, that also takes advantage of scenery to be found in the Pyrenees mountains but this time further north-west towards the town of Pau in the Pyrénées-Atlantiques Department and which began life as a means of serving the construction of a dam for a reservoir that would provide hydro-electric power for the Chemin de fer due Midi (CFM) that later became part of the SNCF. Today the line continues as a tourist ride up to the reservoir on 500mm gauge track for a distance of some 10kms.

The third illustration moves away from the Pyrenees and was issued in 2011 to celebrate the centenary of 'Train des Pignes', a name derived from the pinecones,

once used for tinder to start the steam engines. More formally known as the Chemin de fer de Provence the line runs inland for 151kms from Nice on the Cote d'Azure towards the Rhone-Alps and the town of Digne-les-Baines. This is a commercially operated line but a heritage operator also runs on part of the line and this stamp manages to show both eras.

The final stamp was issued in 1996 to mark the centenary of the Ajaccio-Vizzavona line on the island of Corsica in the Mediterranean. Corsica is a mountainous island, a mix of stylish coastal towns, dense forest and craggy peaks (Monte Cinto is the highest). It has been part of France since 1768, but retains a distinct Italian culture.

The first line of the Chemin de fer de la Corse opened in 1888 and was quickly extended to provide a network that today reaches from Ajaccio in the south to Bastia and Calvi in the north and is operated using diesel multiple units of varying ages, many being early models of classical French origin.

Germany's postal history had a tumultuous time following the Second World War. The national postal authority was split into two nations: East (Known as DDR) and West, whilst West Berlin also had their own Post Office as did, for a short while in 1947-8 the Allied Occupation of Berlin – French Zone. Thankfully they all came together on Germany's re-unification in 1990.

Chosen for illustration are a series of stamps issued by the DDR between 1980-84 that covered some of the large number of narrow-gauge lines that survived in that region due to the slower economic progress than that of most of western Europe, where motorised transport swept almost all before it. These stamps are issued in very attractive se-tenant strips and treat us to not only the locomotives but also rolling stock and a little map of the line. Happily,

Schmalspurbahnen in der DDR

20 DDR

Bad Doberan-
Ostseebad Kühlungsborn ; Spurweite 900 mm
1980

Schmalspurbahnen in der DDR

35 DDR

Bad Doberan-
Ostseebad Kühlungsborn ; Spurweite 900 mm
1980

Schmalspurbahnen in der DDR

20 DDR

Traditionsbahn
Radebeul · Radeburg ; Spurweite 750 mm
1980

Schmalspurbahnen in der DDR

25 DDR

Traditionsbahn
Radebeul · Radeburg ; Spurweite 750 mm
1980

Schmalspurbahnen in der DDR

5 DDR

Putbus – Göhren ;
Spurweite 750 mm
1981

Schmalspurbahnen in der DDR

20 DDR

Putbus – Göhren ; Spurweite 750 mm
1981

Schmalspurbahnen in der DDR

5 DDR

Freital – Kurort Kipsdorf ; Spurweite 750 mm
1981

Schmalspurbahnen in der DDR

15 DDR

Freital – Kurort Kipsdorf ; Spurweite 750 mm
1981

Schmalspurbahnen in der DDR

15 DDR

Wernigerode · Nordhausen ;
Spurweite 1000 mm
1983

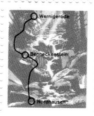

Schmalspurbahnen in der DDR

20 DDR

Wernigerode · Nordhausen ; Spurweite 1000 mm
1983

all these lines survive in one form or another, either as preservation projects or commercial operations taking advantage of their heritage status.

Austria is a country renowned for its mountainous terrain where the building of narrow gauge railways was able to more easily cope with the twists and turns needed to navigate the many parts of the country that standard gauge lines would have found great difficulty reaching – and at great expense.

Today known as Post AG, the Austrian postal authority has a long history of celebrating its transport legacy on its stamps, going back as far as 1923, and in recent times has regularly issued stamps to a standard format featuring both the national system as well as many of the smaller lines and the charm of these narrow gauge lines is

beautifully illustrated by this set of three stamps issued in 1998 to celebrate the centenaries of the Ybbstalbahn, the Postlingbergbahn and the Pinzgaubahn.

Of two more stamps, both issued in 2007, the first one shows a class U, 0-6-2t locomotive synonymous with many of the 760mm gauge Austrian narrow gauge lines and in this case on the Bregenzerwaldbahn, (the Bregenza Forest Railway), a flourishing preserved line that originally served an area in the north west of the country. Notice that addition of afforestation in the illustration.

The brown electric locomotive ran on the Mariazellerbahn, another 760mm gauge line from St. Polten to the Styrian pilgrimage centre of Mariazell in the south-east of the country that was opened in stages between 1898 and 1907. Today the railway is operated by Niederösterreichische Verkehrsorganisationsgesellschaft m.b.H, more commonly known as NÖVOG, owned by the provincial government. These ancient locomotives were extensively rebuilt with new bodies that gave them a much more modern appearance and only in 2015 were they retired when new modern stock was delivered.

FFA-Mareich / Bild 2   2005   Reihe 1099

ÖSTERREICH €0.55

The final stamp is an example of Post AG's Personalisierte Marke, their facility to produce stamps to the purchaser's own personal subject, not just railway subjects but whatever takes your fancy; the author has even seen nudes on these stamps. This particular example shows one the same electric locomotives of the Mariazellerbahn in its rebuilt form.

Further east is **Hungary** where today there are believed to be in the region of twenty narrow gauge lines, or little railways (kisvasut) that are the last vestiges of Hungary's once extensive narrow-gauge network that once covered more than 4,000km of track. Like so many lines once within the Austro-Hungarian empire, these used the 760mm track gauge and the stamps illustrated here show some items of rolling stock characteristic of the country.

AFRICA

This continent that straddles the Equator and both the Tropics of Cancer and Capricorn was not to the forefront of railway development; in fact, the first lines were established in Alexandria, Egypt, in 1852 with an eye on trade with Europe. Railways were also built with a view to transporting troops rapidly in times of war, whilst in almost all countries, Europeans intent on exploiting the continent's natural resources or otherwise profiting from their investment financed and built most of its railways. Look through the following illustrations and you will find a direct link back to one of several of Europe's most adventurous countries and their early pioneering capitalists.

The first stamps I have chosen to illustrate come from the west-African state of **Cote D'Ivoire** (or Ivory Coast in English) that gained independence from the French in 1960 and today the population of just over 20 million predominantly retains the French language.

The country's railway system was built during the period of French influence to a gauge of 1 metre, with the initial intention of connecting the port of Abidjan with Ouagadougou, the capital of Burkina Faso. In 1995, it was estimated that the national network extended to in excess

of 600km. In October 2010, the government announced plans to build a 737km line which would link the port of San Pedro to mines in the west of the country.

The **Republic of Chad** is a land-locked country to the south of Libya and west of Sudan and the fifth largest country in Africa, its capital being N'djamena. Although there has never been a national rail system in the country, there have been many such proposals and therefore the publication of this set of stamps has to be taken as simple and colourful illustrations for their national stamps. Colourful indeed is their pink, light blue and green shades representing machines built in America and Europe. Of particular interest is the Pechot-Bourdon articulated locomotive on the 150f stamp being a close relative of the Fairlie design made famous by the Ffestiniog Railway in North Wales. They were a French design for use in the trenches of the First World-War, built in large numbers both in Europe and by Baldwin

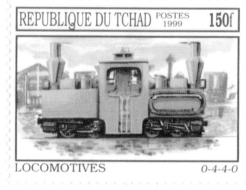

of America who had the capacity to produce large numbers of engines and at very short notice. Unfortunately for modern historians and railway enthusiasts, there are only two known survivors, both immobile in museums, as a great many were destroyed by putting a hand-grenade into the firebox to render them useless to the oncoming enemy!

From **Togo** comes a very enigmatic but delightful stamp produced in 1984 as part of a set depicting various railways in Africa. This minisheet shows a tiny carriage,

presumably used to carry railway executives or dignitaries, as the first train to Dakar, Senegal. Mule power like this must have been seen all over the globe at one time or another.

This country, again in the same general area of western Africa, did have its own railways system from 1905, built to the metre gauge as was the norm for railways then under German colonial power but it fell into disuse by 1999.

Another country to fall under the colonial power of Germany in 1884 was **South West Africa**, although in 1915, South Africa took control until 1990 when the country gained independence and was renamed Namibia. The country has a population of 2.1million people and mining for gem diamonds, uranium, gold, silver, and base metals form the basis of its economy and the principle *raison-d'etre* for railways. The large, arid Namib Desert is known to have been established for millennia and meets the Atlantic Ocean to the west. A more inhospitable landing could barely be imaginable, as attested to by the numerous wrecks to be seen, and has resulted in Namibia being overall one of the

1985 600mm Schmalspur J J van Ellinckhuijzen

J J van Ellinckhuijzen 600mm Feldspur 1985

J J van Ellinckhuijzen 600mm Narrow Gauge 1985

1985 600mm Smalspoor J J van Ellinckhuijzen

least densely populated countries in the world.

These stamps, issued in 1985, illustrate some of the German built locomotives, the 12c is particularly interesting in that it shows a Zwilling-type locomotive. This German word translates as 'twin', nicely explaining the concept, as here there is little more than two small tank-engines, back-to-back with a common floor-plate so that both could be controlled by one crew, an early answer to the problem of coping with increasing loads on light, curving track, for which various forms of articulation also developed.

Moving east, a little explanation is perhaps required for the countries named on these next stamps. **Kenya**, **Uganda**, **Tanganyika** (KUT) was the name on postage stamps made for use in these British colonies that ultimately became independent, the latter country adopting the name Tanzania. Their stamps were used between 1935 and 1963 by the joint postal service of the three colonies, the East African Posts and Telecommunications Administration.

Even after independence, the new separate nations continued to use the KUT stamps and they remained valid for postage until 1977.

Alongside this was the East African Railways and Harbours Corporation that operated railways and harbours in East Africa from 1948 to 1977. It was formed in 1948 for the new East African High Commission by merging the Kenya and Uganda Railways and Harbours with the Tanganyika Railway into a common metre-gauge operation, and these 1971 stamps illustrate a cross-section of the motive-power used in these countries. Also shown is a 1988 stamp from Uganda, after its independence in 1966, and shows a similar locomotive now carrying the title EAR or East African Railways and clearly shows direct lineage with previous types.

The final image of stamps in Africa shows a minisheet of stamps issued by the **South African** Post Office in 2010 to celebrate the 150th anniversary of the first railway in the country, about two miles long, linking the town of Durban with Harbour Point, opened by the Natal Railway Company on 26 June 1860. Since then, the railway system has grown into South Africa's principle transport provider and today extends to some 12,000-route miles principally on 3ft 6in gauge track. As these stamps show, the volume of usage and size of the locomotives and trains does not sit comfortably in the narrow gauge category but is no-less impressive for that.

SOUTH AFRICAN RAILWAYS 150

2010.06.25

710485
710486
710488

NATAL 1860	SOUTH AFRICA	NGG 16 1937	SOUTH AFRICA
R2.40 HEIN BOTHA 2010		R2.40 HEIN BOTHA 2010	
CLASS 24 1948	SOUTH AFRICA	CLASS 25 1953	SOUTH AFRICA
R2.40		R2.40 HEIN BOTHA 2010	
GMA/M 1954	SOUTH AFRICA	CLASS 35 1974	SOUTH AFRICA
R2.40 HEIN BOTHA 2010		R2.40 HEIN BOTHA 2010	
CLASS 9E 1978	SOUTH AFRICA	CLASS 26 1981	SOUTH AFRICA
R2.40 HEIN BOTHA 2010		R2.40	
CLASS 19E 2009	SOUTH AFRICA	GAUTRAIN 2010	SOUTH AFRICA
R2.40 HEIN BOTHA 2010		R2.40	

ASIA

For those interested in railways, then **India** has to be on everyone's bucket list of things to do before they die; the author's list has this country at the top, whether for the astonishing volumes carried by the principal state-owned carriers on both local and inter-city lines now almost all using the gauge of 5ft 6in, or the now almost totally departed narrow gauge lines that criss-crossed the country as secondary feeders. But India is also famous for several other narrow gauge lines built to transport those suffering from the oppressive heat of Indian cities to the relative cool of the hill stations and I have used these stamps to illustrate the diversity still to be seen.

Unquestionably the most famous is the Darjeeling Himalayan Railway line also known as the 'Toy Train', a 2ft (610mm) gauge) line that runs between New Jalpaiguri and Darjeeling in the Indian state of West Bengal. Built between 1879 and 1881, the railway is about 78km (48 miles) long. Its elevation level varies from about 100m (328ft) at New Jalpaiguri to about 2,200m (7,218ft) at Darjeeling.

CENTENARY OF DARJEELING HIMALAYAN RAILWAY 1982

100 Years of Kalka - Shimla Railway

The 2r85 stamp of 1982 beautifully illustrates one such train with the Himalayan mountain range behind whilst the 6r00 stamp of 1993 illustrates one of the ubiquitous 'B'-class engines, built both in England and by Baldwin in the USA.

Today, the railway is classified as a World Heritage Site by UNESCO and enthusiastically supported by the

British-based Darjeeling Himalayan Railway Society, but the railway's future has been as precarious as some of its mountain track for many years and those contemplating a visit are recommended to take advantage of one of the tours offered by various travel companies.

The 1993 set of stamps also illustrate the Neral-Matheran, the Nilgiri Mountain and the Kalka-Shimla lines. The latter is a 2ft 6in (762mm) line in North-West India, travelling along a mostly mountainous route linking the two towns that bear its name and known for dramatic views of the hills and surrounding villages. The line was completed in 1898, Shimla being the summer capital of India during the British Raj and the 5 rupee stamp was issued in 1998 to celebrate the line's centenary.

Off India's southeastern coast lies the island nation of **Sri Lanka**, formerly known as Ceylon. Its diverse landscapes range from rainforest and arid plains to highlands and sandy beaches and it is famed for its ancient Buddhist ruins, including the fifth century citadel Sigiriya, with its palace and frescoes. The city of Anuradhapura, Sri Lanka's ancient capital, has many ruins dating back more than 2,000 years.

Today a substantial network of broad-gauge (5ft 6in) lines operates but the narrow 2ft 6in gauge lines all perished some years ago, either abandoned altogether or converted to broad gauge, where sometimes a section retained a third rail for narrow gauge running in the early days. This has allowed occasional use by such rolling stock right up to the present day, featuring two items that appear on these colourful 2011 stamps and apart from two broad gauge locomotives are first of all an extremely rare survivor of British attempts to produce a self-powered railway carriage, in this case a combined effort between the Sentinel company of Shrewsbury and Metropolitan Cammell of Birmingham. Adjacent is a 4-6-4 tank locomotive of class J1, produced by the Hunslet Engine Company of Leeds in 1924.

"Viceroy Special" Steam Locomotive B8 240

"Viceroy Special" Locomotive B2 213

Sentinel Camel Steam Rail Car V2 331

Narrow Gauge Steam Locomotive J1 220

Moving further east our collection of stamps draws us to **Thailand**, known for tropical beaches, opulent royal palaces, ancient ruins and ornate temples displaying figures of Buddha. In Bangkok, the capital, an ultramodern cityscape rises next to quiet canal-side communities and the iconic temples of Wat Arun, Wat Pho and the Emerald Buddha Temple (Wat Phra Kaew).

Its railway system was originally founded in 1890 as the standard gauge Royal State Railways of Siam, the original name of the country. Other lines were built to metre-gauge and eventually all lines – extending today to over 2,500 route-miles – were converted to this gauge. Tragically, like British Railways of old, this state run railway has long been starved of investment and management, but our little selection of stamps gives us a cheerful glimpse of times-past.

Taiwan, formerly known as Formosa, (from the Portuguese – *Ilha Formosa* or Beautiful Island) is an island some 112 miles off the south-eastern coast of mainland China across the Taiwan Strait. The eastern two-thirds are dominated by mountainous areas that are heavily forested and home to a diverse range of wildlife. To work these forest regions, the Alishan Forest Railway was built, starting in 1912, by the Japanese interests as a 50 mile network of 2ft 6in narrow gauge railways running up to the popular mountain resort of Alishan in Chiayi County and has now become a tourist attraction with unique Z-shaped switchbacks, 50 tunnels, and over 77 wooden bridges and has always been famous for its American built Shay articulated locomotives. Illustrated are two stamps issued in 1992 as well as a mini-sheet aimed at tourists that was issued in 2012 to commemorate the line's centenary.

THE PACIFIC REGION

ominating this area, of course, is **Australia**, officially the Commonwealth of Australia, and in mentioning this country in the narrow gauge context it is impossible not to think immediately of the Puffing Billy Railway, a 2ft 6in narrow gauge heritage railway between Belgrave and Gembrook, close to Melbourne in the State of Victoria, through the forests, fern gullies and farmlands of the magnificent Dandenong Ranges. It is the major part of the line which opened on 18 December 1900 and operated over 18.2 miles (29km) until 1953, when a landslide blocked the track and, because of operating losses, the line was closed the following year.

Public interest resulted in the formation of the Puffing Billy Preservation Society that runs the line today. The first-day cover the author has chosen to illustrate the line with was issued in 2015 and shows one of the well-known American-style locomotives. The original ones were purchased from Baldwin of America but subsequently multiplied by Australian

industry. Notice also the children sitting facing outward from the coach sides, a habit shown in many photographs of the line but likely to give Health and Safety experts cataclysmic episodes anywhere else.

New Zealand is, like Australia, a part of the world that I have never managed to get to, so it is fortunate that I came across this mini-sheet produced by the Ferrymead Heritage Park, barely five miles from the centre of Christchurch on the country's South Island, as a series of Railway Letter fee stamps showing off some of the history of New Zealand's railway past built principally to a gauge of 3ft 6in. The park features an early 1900s (Edwardian) township, with exhibits such as houses, a cinema, school classroom, church, jail, railway station and much more.

There is also a large array of heritage museums and displays that are often open for viewing, particularly on Sundays. These museums are owned and operated by individual societies. Their own volunteer workers restore and display their collections, such as tractors, fire engines, aeroplanes, trams, trains, theatrical operations, mini rail, model trains, radios and photography etc.

About 750 miles east of Brisbane, Australia lie the beautiful islands of **New Caledonia**, or as it is today officially known, Nouvelle Caledonie, a French territory comprising dozens of islands in the South Pacific. It is known for its palm-lined beaches and marine-life-rich lagoon. A massive barrier reef surrounds the main island, Grand Terre, a major scuba-diving destination. The capital, Nouméa, is home to French-influenced restaurants and luxury boutiques selling Parisian fashions.

The Nouméa-Païta railway was the only railway line serving New Caledonia. It was opened in December 1914 between Nouméa and Païta. The 3ft (914mm) narrow gauge tracks of the railway ran 18miles between the two cities. Although it closed in 1940, American troops rebuilt most

of it for their own logistical needs during the Second World War though it did not last long and today there are but few reminders the line ever existed. Other minor railways have been seen on these islands for the exploitation of mineral deposits and the stamps shown here illustrate this operation as well as giving us a few clues about the Païta line.

Continuing our journey east will eventually bring us to the islands of **Fiji**, a country in the South Pacific that is an archipelago of more than 300 islands. It is famed for rugged landscapes, palm-lined beaches and coral reefs with clear lagoons. Its major islands, Viti Levu and Vanua Levu, contain most of the population. Viti Levu is home to the capital, Suva.

The growing of sugar cane goes back to 1862 and as a cash crop it grew to be the major export commodity of the country, expanded by the Australian company Colonial

SUGAR MILLS FREE PASSENGER TRAIN

SUGAR MILLS DIESEL LOCO.no.1

Sugar Refining Company (CSR) but taken over by the Fiji Sugar Corporation – today the country's largest public company – in 1972. A railway system to serve the industry was first established in 1882 and the CSR developed it into a 2ft gauge system with in excess of 400 miles of line. Whilst today the industry and its railway are some- what diminished, it does continue to flourish, bringing much needed employment and revenue to these beautiful islands. So proud are the islanders of their little trains that four distinct issues of stamps have featured them, a solitary stamp in 1954 shown in the Series Introduction as well as this colourful set issued in 1975.

Interestingly, the steam locomotives featured were part of a large number built for the CSR in both their Australian and Fijian businesses by the Leeds builder Hudswell Clarke and whilst a small number have been preserved and returned to use for heritage operation, two from Fiji have been returned to the United Kingdom to operate on the private Statfold Barn line in Staffordshire.

THE AMERICAS

The author confesses that in all his years as a philatelist he has come across very little worth illustrating in this volume from the major nations of North and South America even though there are many flourishing preservation organisations and even a few narrow gauge railways where the distinction between conventional revenue earning operators established many years ago to provide public transport and today's heritage operation has become blurred. One cover has been picked, however, to illustrate one of the perhaps not quite so well-known lines in Colorado and that is the Uintah Railway which was a small 3ft narrow gauge railroad company in Utah and Colorado in the United States. It was constructed to carry Gilsonite, a naturally-occurring form of asphalt used on roads that provided most of its operating revenues but it operated as a common carrier from 1904 to 1939,

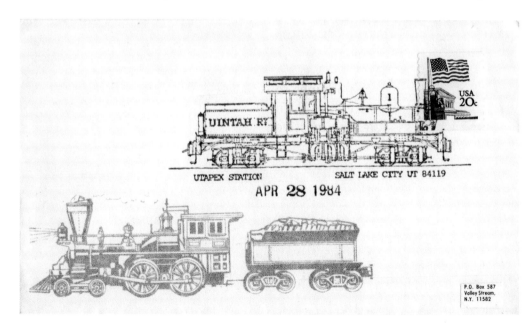

also carrying passengers, mail, express, and other cargoes including sheep and wool. When a public library was built in Dragon in 1910, the Uintah Railway agreed to deliver library books free of charge to and from any borrower along its route. Many of the area's ranchers and miners took advantage of the opportunity.

The cover I have chosen to illustrate shows a special franking that gives us a good outline drawing of a Shay articulated steam engine that had three cylinders mounted on the right hand-side frame and connected to bevel gears on each axle by a series of shafts, making the locomotive ideally suited to pulling relatively heavy loads on indifferent track with sinuous curves and stiff grades. This particular engine is not one of the biggest such engines, as others would extend to four bogies, all connected to the same cylinders by further extensions to the line-shafting.

Happily, though, some of the smaller nations particularly in Central America and the islands in that region are not quite so bashful and I will start with **Belize**, a nation on the eastern coast of Central America with a northern border with Mexico, the Caribbean Sea shorelines to the east and dense jungle to the west. Offshore, the massive Belize Barrier Reef, dotted with hundreds of low-lying islands called cayes, hosts rich marine life. Belize was known as British Honduras until 1981, when it gained independence, but remains a member of the British Commonwealth with Her Majesty the Queen as its monarch and head of state.

Belize enjoyed several different and unconnected railways that were used for the transportation of products ranging from bananas, sugar cane to lumber, operated

BELIZE CAPEX'96 75c

MAHOGANY LOG TRAIN
IS HAULED BY A HUNSLET
0-6-0 SIDE TANK ENGINE No 4

BELIZE CAPEX'96 60c

ENGINE No1 LEAVES STANN CREEK STATION

as purely internal lines transporting these goods for processing and then to the docks for shipment overseas. Companies such as Stann Creek Railway and the Gallon Jug Hillbank Railway used equipment as diverse as small British-built tank engines and rather larger Shay articulated machines used to haul timber.

The stamps shown here were issued in 1996 with the Capex '96 logos and signified a large philatelic exhibition in Toronto, Canada, in that year at which a great many nations exhibited their stamps and all displaying the same logo. The subject of the stamps themselves feature the 3ft 6in gauge Stann Creek Railway built by British interest to haul bananas from 1911 to 1937, when the crop ceased to be grown in that part of the country.

Cuba, of course, will need little introduction, famous for its cigars, classical culture and American motor cars maintained today just as they were built in the 1930s, '40s and '50s, actually a necessity because of the impossible trading position the country finds itself in, even though as these words are written the 'ice' between this country and its bigger neighbour appears to be melting fast. Well remembered is the country's Communist

Cuba correos 2000 65

1919 ALCO 2-8-0
EXPO.FILAT.INT. LONDRES 2000

Cuba correos 2000　75

1925 Alco 2-8-2
EXPO.FILAT.INT. LONDRES 2000

Cuba correos 2000　15

1912 Baldwin 2-8-0
EXPO.FILAT.INT. LONDRES 2000

Cuba correos 2000　5

1882 Baldwin 0-6-0
EXPO.FILAT.INT. LONDRES 2000

Cuba correos 2000　10

1895 Baldwin 2-8-0
EXPO.FILAT.INT. LONDRES 2000

leader, the late Fidel Castro, whilst some will also remember the 'Cuban Missile Crisis' of October 1962 that really did not directly involve Cuba but brought the world to the edge of a nuclear conflict.

Its railways, too, depend upon the ingenuity of Cuban engineers to keep in service rolling stock from a previous era and the country's postal administration known as Cuba Postal are happy to celebrate their continuing heritage and this set is another one to mark a philatelic exhibition, this time in London in 2000, and apart from two standard-gauge locomotives shows three early Baldwin-built locomotives used principally on the 2ft 6in gauge railways that served the sugar cane fields of the island.

Antigua is one of the Leeward Islands in the Eastern Caribbean region and the main island of the country of

Antigua and Barbuda that became an independent state within the British Commonwealth in 1981. After Admiral Nelson arrived in 1784 and set up English Harbour in one of the islands many natural harbours, tourists from throughout the world have been coming here ever since.

Nelson was, however, preceded by Sir Christopher Codrington who, in 1684, came to see if the island could support large-scale sugar cultivation as was already flourishing throughout the Caribbean. This was indeed the case and the industry grew so much that slaves were

Diesel Locomotive No. 15

Steam Locomotive hauling Sugar-cane

Narrow-gauge Steam Locomotive

brought over from Africa to cut and process the crop and it is these people who today make-up the majority of the Island's population. In the 20th Century the industry declined and it was a political decision to concentrate the nation's resources on tourism that saw the abandonment of sugar production that, together with its railway, closed in 1972/73.

In 1981 this set of stamps was issued to mark the legacy of the industry and its small railway, the 30-in. (762mm) gauge network stretched out in all directions eventually reaching over 50 miles in length. An attempt to operate a tourist service dubbed 'The Sunshine Shu Shu' using steam loco No. 5 GEORGE and five converted cane cars in 1968/69 and again in 1972/73 failed.

The majority of the steam locomotives used were built in Great Britain by Kerr Stuart of Stoke-on-Trent, probably the most well-known today being No.7, JOAN that now runs on the Welshpool & Llanfair line in mid-Wales. The diesel No. 10 as illustrated on the mini-sheet was a product of the Hudson-Hunslet company, (a joint venture by two well-known Leeds based businesses) and is now also believed to be in the UK.

Going further east from the principal parts of the Americas, we find the **Falkland Islands** (Islas Malvinas), a remote South Atlantic archipelago (about 300 miles east of the South American mainland). With rugged terrain and cliff-lined coasts, its hundreds of islands and islets are home to sheep farms and abundant birdlife and a human population now exceeding 2,500. The capital, Stanley, sits on East Falkland, the largest island.

Controversy exists over the Falklands' discovery and subsequent colonisation by Europeans. At various times, the islands have had French, British, Spanish and Argentine settlements. Britain reasserted its rule in 1833 and although Argentina maintains its claim to the islands, they remain resolutely part of Great Britain.

Some initial skirmishes at the beginning of the First World War demonstrated the need for improved communications with the UK, so an extremely powerful 'spark transmitter' was built that required formidable amounts of power and a 2ft gauge railway known as the Camber Railway had to be built to transport all the equipment needed the 3.5miles from the Navy jetty near Stanley out to where the mast was built, and subsequently to provide the coal-fired power station with its fuel. Development of the wireless valve made the transmitter obsolete and by the mid-1920s, the railway had fallen into disuse with the two locomotives, its wagons and much other equipment unceremoniously dumped off the end of the navy pier! In the 1980s, the locomotives and some other equipment were salvaged and are believed to be still in store so that one day, perhaps, something might be made presentable for future generations to see.

There have been two sets of stamps issues by the Falkland Islands postal authorities and the author has chosen this rather charming set from 1985 to show the two little 'Wren' type locomotives built by Kerr, Stuart & Co. Ltd of Stoke-on-Trent as well as some of the other stock used.

54ᴾ **Falkland Islands**

SMOKER 3ᴿᴰCLASS   2ᴺᴰ CLASS   1ˢᵀ CLASS   FALKLAND ISLAND EXPRESS

CAMBER RAILWAY 1915-1927

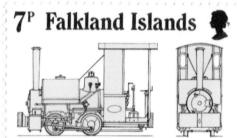

7ᴾ **Falkland Islands**

CAMBER RAILWAY 1915-1927

27ᴾ **Falkland Islands**

CAMBER RAILWAY 1915-1927

22ᴾ **Falkland Islands**

CAMBER RAILWAY 1915-1927

COLLECTING

What makes us collect stamps? Come to think of it – what makes us collect anything? Is there a hoarding instinct in some of us, or all of us? A squirrel hoards nuts for the lean months, whilst at times of national stress we have all seen supermarket shelves emptied quickly; but stamps? Or playing cards? The author has collected various genres of transport models for decades, buses, trains and aircraft in big numbers, but why? There are private collectors of works

of art, the value of their collections are not necessarily monetary but just as likely emotional, and probably not with an eye on an investment. Others will see collecting as a way of reliving their childhood, or an aspect of their life most dear to them.

Parents and grandparents will be familiar with childrens' obsession with collecting cards, maybe of footballers, and here we see the excitement of the chase, to obtain the vital last or rarest one to show off to their school friends and perhaps here we will find the psychology of collecting stamps; the pride in building up a collection, the hunt for the rarity or an 'error', a specialisation in itself, that can vary enormously from a spelling mistake (embarrassing

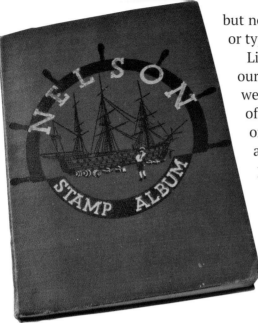

but not unknown) to missing colours or type.

Like collector-cards we saved in our youth, stamp collecting may well start with the fascination of issues from across the globe or from previous eras. A kindly aunt's birthday or Christmas present may see our first album with pages for a great many of the world's nations, and possibly an envelope of mixed stamps, sometimes unused – mint – or maybe used and still on a fragment the envelope.

In the photograph of 'The Nelson' album we see just such an item, un-dated but this teenage owner has made notes on the contents dated 1953-5. The hunt has begun, to piece together the perceived history of that collection as we are led by the

EESTI KITSARÖÖPMELINE RAUDTEE
1896 - 1996
FDC

album with the stamps scattered in all probability all over the dining-room table or the lounge carpet and before long the craving developed, to add to this collection and then to multiply the number of albums needed to accommodate the growing collection until eventually order will need to be established. At that time, the likelihood is that there will be some sort of concentration or specialisation, perhaps on specific countries or regions, or themes such as the subject of this series of books.

A great many stamp collectors concentrate on the country

of their birth or home and build-up a comprehensive history of that nation's stamps into a portfolio of immense prestige that may even include text to provide a commentary or catalogue number. Another speciality is the study of the perforations that surround each stamp for ease of separating from the sheets, their size and hence the number on each edge, and to damage these devalues the stamp as much as a rip or thinning of the paper itself due to careless removal from its backing or hinges. As postal authorities modernised and became more mechanised, stamps had watermarks added or phosphor strips which bore vital information. And then there is the collector with an eye on the investment, for undoubtedly a great many stamps reward the serious collector very well and there are organisations that offer advice for the committed investor. Reading one of the established magazines on our subject will enlighten some and surprise others.

LOOKING AFTER STAMPS

That such a big industry, or some would say profession, has grown out of the love of a little piece of paper with gum on the back might be hard to credit; but the obsession with the minutiae of the subject can sometimes seem out of all proportion.

Our Aunt's birthday present gave the young and budding philatelist the encouragement to either glue those precious stamps within the dotted squares provided or with wisdom found the little clear hinges that preserved them at least temporarily in place. But today both these habits are discredited as they effect the stamp itself, for today the serious collector goes to incredible lengths to preserve each individual stamp in as near as possible the condition it left the printer in. First of all one should never touch the stamp itself, grease and other contaminants will over time degrade the surface whilst clumsy fingers can quite easily crease or tear the delicate paper and perforations; so acquisition of specialised tweezers like the pair shown here are a good idea, then take the trouble to look at the various types of album available.

Most will be ring-binders ready to accept the many different pages available. Some of these pages will have clear strips of varying depths to keep stamps secure but visible whilst others are available pre-printed with details of the country of origin and the specific issue to which it refers and it only remains for the owner to place his treasured morsel of paper behind special clear envelopes cut to size and ready for attaching to the designated space. Many will produce his or her own leaves, suitably annotated and presumably preserved in beautiful albums bound in leather. Many collectors exhibit their work at well-known

exhibitions in venues across the globe and their work is often lauded amongst their piers.

Finally. The collector must remember the bible of the stamp world – the catalogue. Here one will find a huge coming-together of stamps one would not otherwise dream of, listed in copious detail by country and date to give a firm basis to any collection. Usually a value will also be provided although one has to treat these with a little caution, as this is totally dependant on condition and the vagaries of market forces. Considering the detail and how up-to-date one needs to be, these can be acquired for a few pounds or up to several hundreds for the most comprehensive; that from Stanley Gibbons stretching to several volumes at a cost running into the hundreds of pounds; and whilst these are up-dated regularly only the obsessive or professional will want to replace them regularly.